YIN♪YANG
BYTES

Wayfarer & Elfin

in gratitude to
YOU

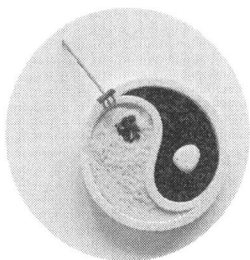

thank you for being

Yin Yang Bytes
data bursts on
the nature of origin...

... shared, set down, planted, to tickle and take root where deep down knowing resides; to fluently expand understanding, aligning mind through effortless unlearning, uniting the magical and the ordinary to unleash the extra-ordinary.

Embark upon a delightful journey with these words and images as they flow toward a natural conclusion of wholeness - sprouting ideas in consciousness, igniting mind, opening unseen spaces until clarity unfolds, fusing being and doing, gathering the jewels of life into noble-hearted living. A sense of completeness rising - the perfect launchpad for living in this multifaceted transient 'instant' new world.

YIN/YANG
BYTES

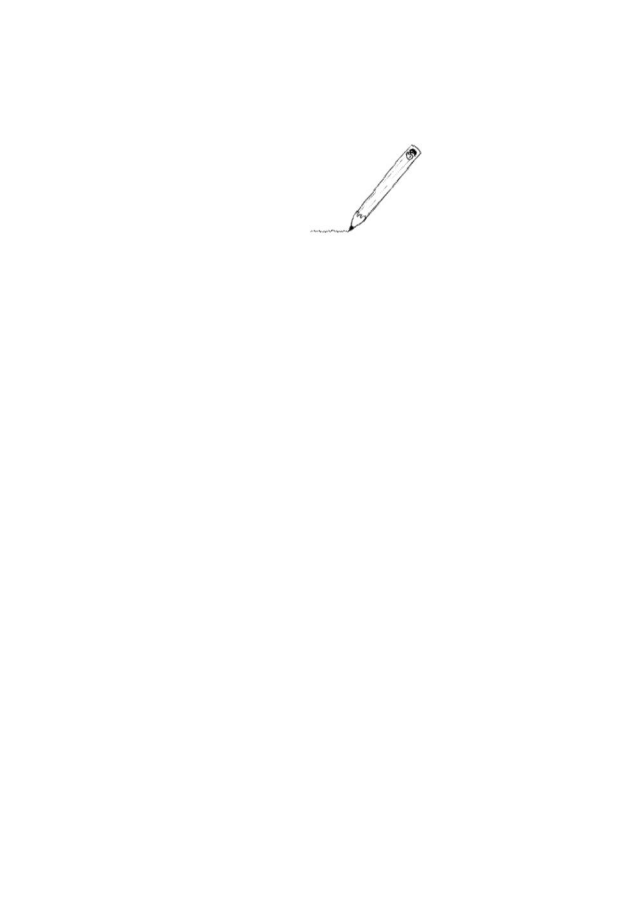

the eternal passing through the
temporal
breath - spirited wind

sunlit seaspray inside
formless moving in form

O

empowering endlessly
when allowed free passage
light switched 'on'

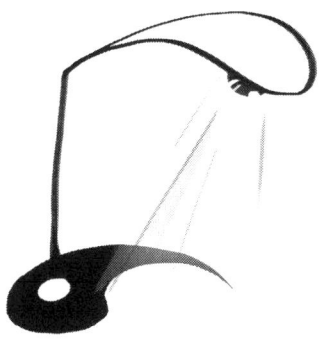

in seeking to acquire one cannot
      recognise

when want drifts without idea of
loss or gain
      to what end unknown

desire arises

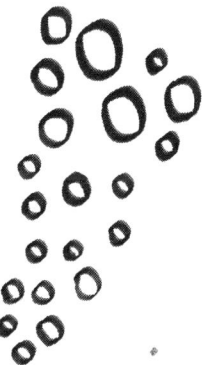

      translucent bubbles set free

      transforming all

physical joins creation
in a non-time bound way

as one in being
no intervening dialogue
no middleman
yet distinguished in relationship

as the wave creates of itself

unique potency expressed

movement initiated
life expressed

links time with timeless
condenses formless with form
joins named with nameless

stir forth
express
what began outside of time in time

wind afoot in the treetops

cause and effect as one

recall

permeable energy patterning
of origin
physical and non physical
both embodied and disembodied

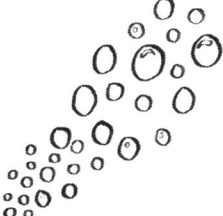

iridescent spray in flight with wind

many variations
one source

false representation

either this 🌀
 or that ☯
breeds illusion
separate parts

without facts -
 knowing ☯
a non particular state outside
of time

when by nature attributeless

coal is easily diamond

opposites exist as different aspects of one whole

yield the tension of opposing opposites

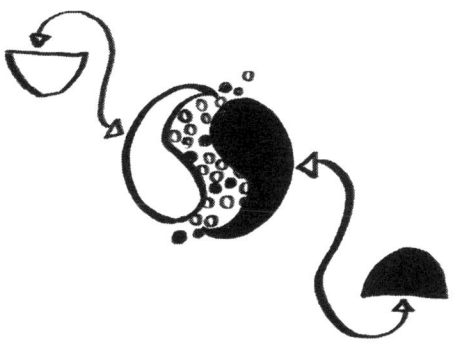

mending the rift
mix let mingle
requires both pushing and pulling
form to formless
formless to form

original nature of form dwells beyond
the mists of duality

observe wave  and
particle ●

at once

energy absorbed
released as light

phosphorescence

light in water undefined by
time bound particularity

the mystery in the apparent

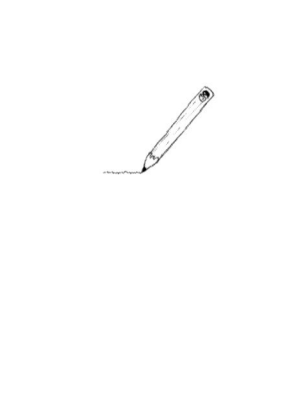

outside systems represent
the made
the already done

systems drawn from union
call patterning of formless
hidden nature

infusing two into motion

day and night as
sunrise
sunset

the hidden present

thought observed
not with ideas already planted
not with projection
nor interpretation

viewed instead atop a mast
sails billowing

ahead clear
horizons

in stillness
observing
all is beheld with all insight

responses already given

listening for meaning already
bestowed

a thought given

vision observed
revelation received
discovery shared

chosen responses ripple like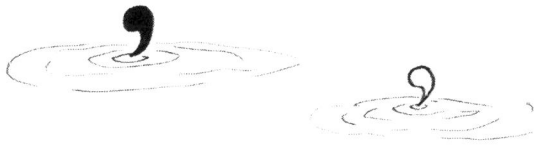
drops reverberating on a clear pond

effortlessly

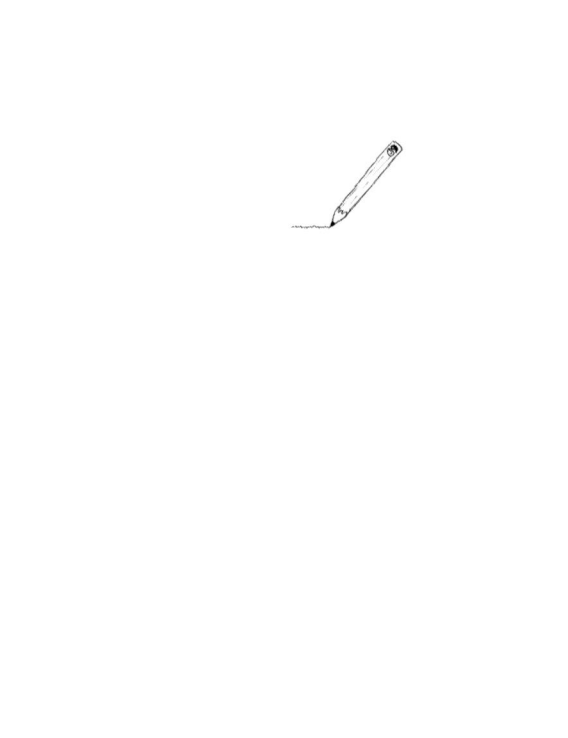

Ideas thoughts in flight

require neither learning
nor accomplishment

● play with the unseen

making seen O

alchemy

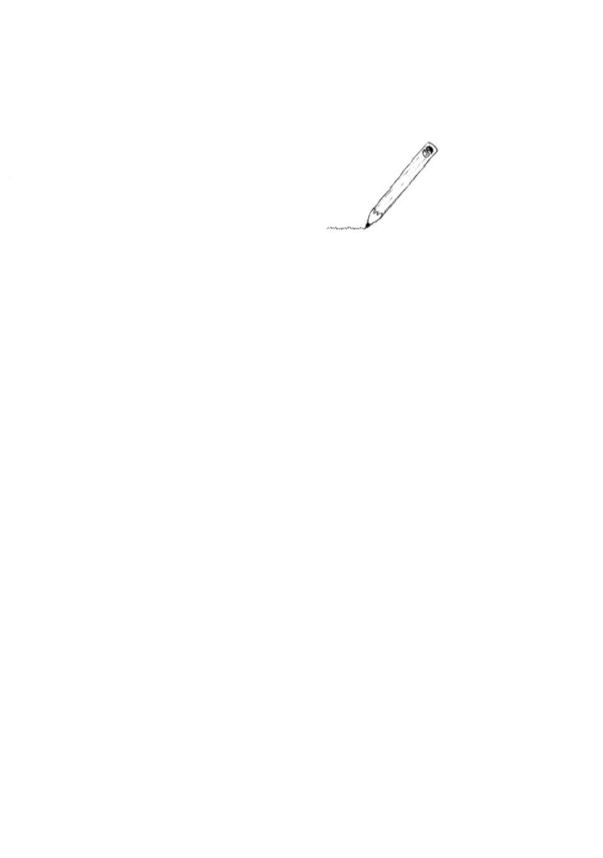

perceiving - learning assumed
to observe is to witness

neutral
empty
a blank screen back lit
infinite

formed yet formless
know thyself without perception

love rising in a building
without frame

'presence'

inspired thought patterning of
acceptance

sacred sense and common
sense serve united
both known and unknown

sunshine in the wave

simple beautiful
form of origin in motion

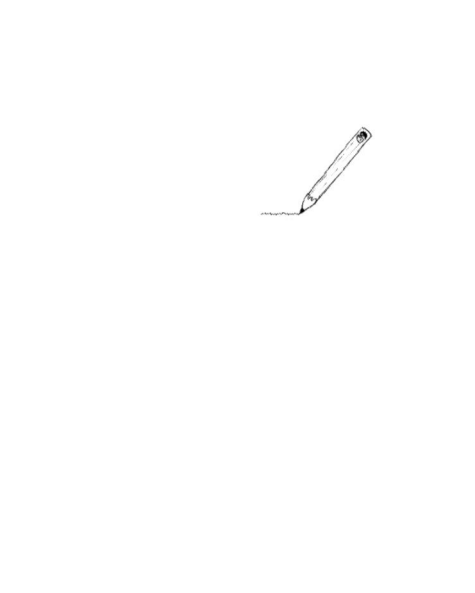

awaken presence
sacred sense -
misty eyes clearing
unable to house fear

a momentary eclipse

portal opens

studies abandoned
vision reclaimed

'breathless'

alchemical catalyst

actively employ expansion
reach beyond

in releasing reverence
like love rising

absorb mystery
like awe
descending

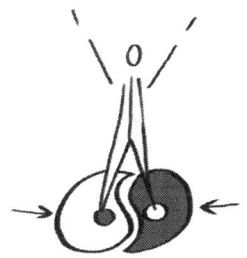

uniting opposites

full flush
no parts missed

flourishing

journeying from image to
'presence'

operate by extension
both
in and out of time
in stillness and in motion

observe the hidden in the present
revealing the beneath behind beyond
finding
form contrary to appearance
being
the apparent in the mysterious
the nameless in the named

physical form
- witness in presence
fusing apparent opposites

the lucid in the dreaming
all seeing
all in-sight
both form and as yet unformed

the green inherent
in the yellow and blue

awareness of eternal
ever-changing everlasting
patterning of form

wholeness actualised
undivided
light and water harmonised
into observable form

rainbow

alchemy accomplished

yin yang
harmony ignited
two become one in relationship

blending of day and night
 edge of dawn
 last line of dusk
equal in measure

one in union
yet individualised
in relationship

effortlessly effectively
expressed

when increase arises
means are provided

yin yang understood
wholehearted
opposing opposites united

arriving departing
absorbing releasing
pushing and pulling

two parts occurring at once
seen and unseen

heatwaves shimmering above
tarmac

hidden majesty revealed

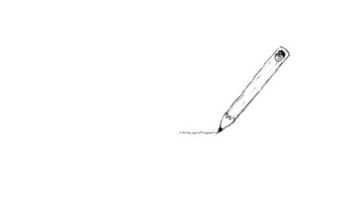

since one cannot be other
one cannot fail

one is
already prepared
already done
already accomplished
substance and source expressed

two can make one
in co-respond-dance

yin
yang in
motion

interrelated
perfected in unison

creation -
gifting attributes to the
attributeless

light reflections sustained
in existence
in union
in tended
suspended in the observable

bath bubbles

the invisible visible

intersession called

  a moment missed
  a heartbeat skipped
  a blank screen lit

interval in ordinary time patterning

focused intent conjured at once
a sudden billowing of sails

source of origin
glimpsed

form of origin patterning

every cell mobilised ignited
as one co-responding-dance

permeable energy
fusing defusing

fireflies in the night sky
glowing 'presence' in form

ideas sailing on a sea of unity
gathering the winds of spirit
passing through the mists of
time

grace envisioned
set down
seasoned
observable

fire sparks set a dancing
amidst a breeze of
understanding
form and intent both
full hearted

continuity
an attribute of relationship not matter
is a present moment event

sacred sense - nameless faculty and
physical sense - named faculties
all in
united

light beams through clouds
parted

well of 'presence'
extra-ordinary now ordinary

stars of the skies
waters of the
ocean
in the
embrace -

field of inspiration
release thinking - active
allow thought - receptive

infinite dew drops atop blades
of grass

meaning given through revelation
heaven sent

source of nature in existence

ever in motion
ever permeable
ever new patterning of form

night sweeps after images of day
in favour of dawn's renewal

seasons of time

replaced with
seasons of regeneration

form-al power

thought coalesced
flooded with intent
set alight in unified focus

a sudden sense-less stillness

an out of ordinary time
pattern interval

view harmonised

intersession

response drawn from the well of origin

gentle raindrops on clear waters

multiple ripples in the lamplight of acceptance

a vision sustained in existence itself in relationship

alchemy sustained

all paths lead to the summit
understanding their nature one alights
at once

mists parted
      peak glimpsed
           residing pathless
stillness

apparent gust of quietude

formless observed passing
      through form whispering the
      song of origin

natural elevation
elevating itself

form of origin song code

formless echoes resoundingly
through the chambers of
form
a choir in movement
with a little giggle permeates
each rung of spines
ladder

ascending

physical and non
physical coalesced
newness
configured

    descending
aligned in motion

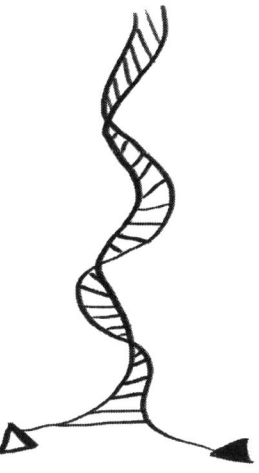

reside
attributeless
natureless
heart and mind all in
at one

chosen thought complete -
a comprehensive patterning
uniquely individuated
expressed
yet undivided

one - no thing to accomplish -
self

treasure actualised

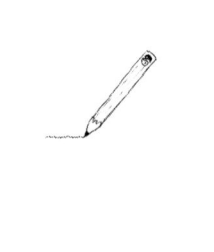

one complete

buoyant on a sea of acceptance

union extended

reaching beyond

harnessing the winds of spirit

coalescing

receiving the wave

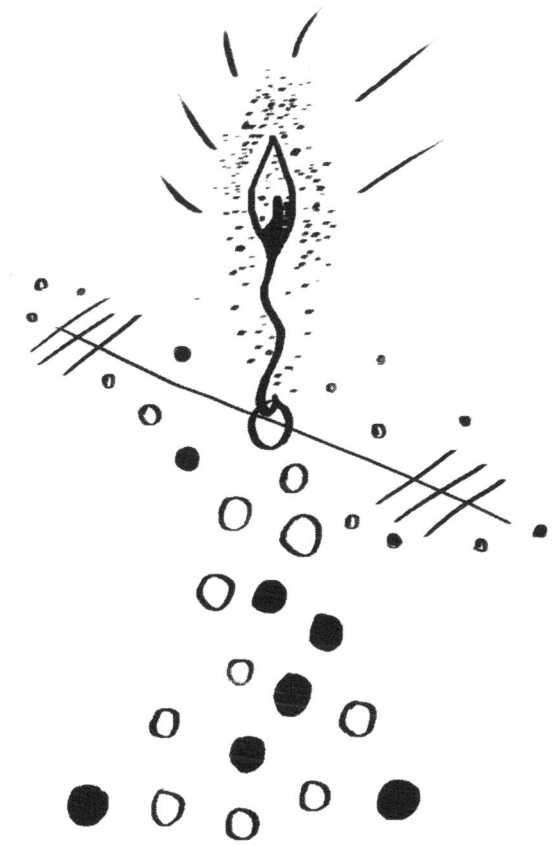

igniting source

transmitting

poised

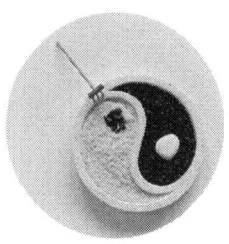

with loving thanks to
the noble hearted ones who
played their part in making
this so:
lahlee · pauline · tara · sara · hedge
and in gratitude to all 'loverly
ones' ♡ who have journeyed
alongside for gifting their
uniqueness and beauty
in 'presence'.

Wayfarer & Elfin

ideas of a different nature

www.wayfarerandelfin.com

Yin Yang Bytes
data bursts on the nature of origin...

Embark upon a delightful journey with these words and images as they flow toward a natural conclusion of wholeness - sprouting ideas in consciousness, igniting mind, opening unseen spaces until clarity unfolds, fusing being and doing, gathering the jewels of life into noble-hearted living. A sense of completeness rising - the perfect launchpad for living in this multi-faceted, transient, 'instant' new world.

"My spiritual journey has been extensive, spanning many years with many teachings. This book however, is something quite different. For me, reading these messages felt like a journey – my journey – filled with wonderful healing energy sent to uplift and teach me on a level I didn't need to consciously understand – and that's gotta be a good thing!"

Sara Mendes da Costa